Responding to Particular Needs at a Precise Moment

Tirana, Albania, March 2015

RISTORANTE

Vitalpharma
RMACI
Ristorante
frymëzuar nga
NATYRA
Bitburger

BIRRA TIRANA

GENI
Valvoline
motor oil

STOP

2005/01/0

The Housing Block as a Framework

Jonas von Lenthe in conversation with Ledian Bregasi on parasitic building in Tirana. The interview took place at Tirana Polis University in March 2015.

Jonas: I have returned to Tirana having developed a fascination for the appearance of its buildings with their informal additions which I saw when I came here previously. I am now trying to explore this fascination, to go beyond the visual and what seems to me to be a romanticising perspective. What is your interest in the informally built structures in Tirana? Why is it part of your study as an architect?

Ledian: I see potential in this spontaneous way of building. It has the potential to adapt to changing conditions of the environment and to respond directly to political, economic or cultural changes. And I want to point out that this potential lies in the city itself, not in the authorities. Of course it is not a solution to every problem the city faces. A city is a complex system and there are no simple answers to this complexity. At the moment what interests me is how in other fields of study simple actions can result in complex behaviours that can respond to big challenges. For example, in computer science, biology or physics you can see that solutions to big problems can be provided by small and autonomous entities that together create complex behaviours. I suppose that the individual inhabitants of the city, even though they are limited in their capacity and their perspective of the whole city, have been able to find solutions on a global scale to global challenges by responding to their particular needs at a precise moment.

Jonas: What is the historical context of this way of building in Albania? Can you talk a little about the time of transition in Albania in terms of the built environment?

Ledian: The situation in Albania in the 1990s was quite complex. After the collapse of the communist system a lot of industries closed. Many people living in nearby smaller cities, where the population was largely employed in these industries, either left Albania or moved to bigger cities, such as Tirana or Durres. As a result, these cities grew rapidly. During the socialist era building projects were exclusively undertaken by the state; there were no private sector initiatives until 1991. The political system had just collapsed and there were no private companies, so people started to build themselves.

Jonas: Is this "parasitic building", so called by you in your article "An Architecture without Architects" (in: *Theory for the Sake of the Theory: ARCHTHEO'11 Conference Proceedings*), still going on in Tirana or has it stopped?

Ledian: I would say the phenomenon for now has stopped. Those illegal additions are very much related to a low enforcement status in the city. Whenever little attention is paid to the administration of the city, for example between the tenures of two mayors, you notice that these illegal additions flourish, but in general it has stopped.

There has also been a process of legalisation of what has been built so far. The first attempt was in 2006, when the government mapped all these illegal buildings and areas in Albania in order to establish a "time zero", after which any structures would be considered illegal. However, there is also a debate whether this legalisation process in fact stimulates illegal building, since legalisation of these buildings every few years may raise an expectation that this legalisation process will occur again and again.

Jonas: What criteria are being applied in order to legalise a building?

Ledian: One of the criteria is the location of the building —the land on which it is built has to be owned by you. If you do not own it, then there are several restrictions and you have to pay a fee to the state. Also, there are areas that are considered off-limits: close to a national road or on the coastline there have been cases in which these buildings have been demolished by the state.

Jonas: When I look at the facade of a socialist housing block in Tirana and its informal modifications the question of authorship always comes to my mind. Are these modifications an example of collective authorship that can lead to a visual language deeply connected to the inhabitants of the city?

Ledian: That is an interesting topic because we have been crossing from one extreme to the other. During socialism we had a habit of mass-producing: building standardised accomodation for "new people", for similar families with similar lives. Even here arises a question of authorship or identity because if you mass-produce buildings, at some point the name of the architect becomes irrelevant. Now we see the other extreme, where there is such diversity that you somehow lose individuality, even though all these additions and informal buildings are different from each other. There is so much noise that you perceive white noise. There have been, at least in Tirana, some sporadic attempts to recruit star architects to make some landmarks in the city. Maybe the authorship cannot be found in the buildings but in a method of planning or a building process that can be reused or refined.

Jonas: You mean like designing certain restrictions or a framework in which the house owner can work toward his or her vision?

Ledian: Yes, as I said, we are passing from one extreme to another. But maybe there is a key to understanding something through this or to find a negotiation point where the creation of a generic framework leaves some degree of freedom and initiative which may be useful for the city. And I am still thinking about your question of authorship—who would be the author then? Would it be the one providing the frame, or the others that fill it in? Another related question is: at what point is a building finished? When you look at pictures of buildings on websites or portfolios of architects, you see that architects tend to take this picture at the very moment when construction is finished but when the building is not yet used. Because after that moment the mere presence of the user changes the status of the building dramatically. However, you could also say that the moment when the design of an object is finished, its life starts.

Returning to Tirana: the interesting part of the modernist, serial buildings is that the full potential of the city was not understood until now, the moment that the inhabitants started to adapt and change the city. So it is not only the potential of the people, but also of this standardised architecture, that allows transformation.

Jonas: Yes, it is very visible. Today you see the old serial buildings and at the same time the fruit of this potential which they had always had.

Ledian: I think these buildings have a quality that was unknown at the time when they were planned and built. Until the moment when a neighbourhood started to be reused and adapted to a new way of living, this quality of the building had yet to be realised.

Jonas: Can you point out concrete examples of this quality?

Ledian: For example, all the ground floors turned from apartments into restaurants or bars: a place where the old people used to get together is now an open bar or a café. But also the apartments themselves were changed, for example by adding a few square feet to turn an apartment for three people into an apartment for a bigger family.

Jonas: What do you think is happening currently in Tirana? The additions might have stopped for now but the city is still changing.

Ledian: One of the definitions of complex systems is that they are difficult to predict. The additions have a limit before they affect the living conditions of the inhabitants. If somebody is building above or behind you and somebody is blocking your view, this tends to create problems. What I am more concerned about is that very few people are analysing or trying to understand something of what has happened and is happening. We have a tendency to erase the past and rebuild from scratch again and again. I think that this behaviour needs not only to be understood in order to prevent it in the future, but we also need to grasp its potential. Let us try to understand what we have done—maybe not all of it was wrong.

Collective Planning and Voluntary Construction

Jonas von Lenthe in conversation with Dritan Mico on socialist Albanian architecture. The interview took place in a café close to Piazza Navona in Rome in March 2016.

Jonas: What is the origin of the typologies of the socialist housing blocks in Tirana?

Dritan: The origin of the socialist-era housing blocks in Albania lays in the very modernist principles of the "Wohnung für das Existenzminimum" (The Minimum Dwelling). These concepts were developed in Frankfurt by architect and city planner Ernst May amongst others and aimed to ensure quality housing in terms of providing fresh air, daylight and hygiene at the lowest possible cost. Socialist housing started in Tirana in 1949 with very basic buildings of two floors. Due to the industrialisation of the country and the urbanisation that went along with it, there was a huge need for accommodation during the first years of socialism.

Jonas: Who was in charge of the design of the housing blocks?

Dritan: The Central Institute of Architecture and Town Planning No. 1 dealt with the design of the dwellings. Its planning practice followed the Soviet Union model and each year, it would launch a new type of a standardised dwelling. As well as this Institute there were also regional offices involved in the design process. These regional offices could for example adapt the facade to the needs of the local climate or follow a regional tradition, for instance, the use of typical material or the shape of the roof, or similar aspects.

Jonas: How was the Central Institute of Architecture and Town Planning No. 1 organised? Was it structured as a collective?

Dritan: Yes, the work was meant to be a collective process. But still there are names of architects that appear often in the plans of housing apartments from that time. During my study of these plans there were three names, that I came across very often: Ibrahim Prushi, Andon Lufi and Gani Strazimiri. These three had all studied abroad and were—after returning to Albania—assigned to design some of the standardised housing types during the first years of the socialist era.

Jonas: Who built the apartment blocks after the Central Institute had planned them?

Dritan: The public construction companies were in charge of erecting the housing blocks. Later, voluntary work became a more and more established practice—it became normal for citizens to dedicate a number of hours to the construction of their future apartments. Voluntary work on a larger scale as a method of housing construction was first applied in 1967, when an earthquake destroyed parts of the existing buildings. Huge parts of the reconstruction were carried out through voluntary work, as there was a strong motivation in the population to help. Also, this self-production method proved to be an efficient tool to keep the cost of housing as low as possible.

Jonas: Are there examples of the use of prefabricated systems in the construction of new buildings?

Dritan: Yes, there are a few examples. Prefabrication methods were introduced to Albania by Chinese engineers in the second half of the 1960s and exclusively applied during the Sino-Albanian allegiance in late 1960s and early 1970s.

Jonas: How high was the standard of an apartment in one of these blocks compared with other Eastern European countries?

Dritan: The standard of the apartments was more or less the same as in other Eastern European countries, but it was common for more people to live in one apartment than it was designed for. Often more than two generations lived together in one apartment. There were long waiting lists, so living there was considered a privilege. The distribution of housing was also a way to manage the population: since the state controlled the distribution of dwellings, as a consequence the state also had control over inland migration and urbanisation, as well as the population density of Tirana and all other towns.

Jonas: Was there an exchange of ideas and methods between Albanian architects and architects from other countries?

Dritan: Until the 1950s there was a flow of ideas, due to the presence of engineers and architects from former Eastern Bloc countries in Albania. Also, during the first years of the socialist era most Albanian architects were educated abroad. However—aside from a very sporadic transfer with Chinese engineers—this exchange with other countries came to an end with the worsening of relations between the Socialist Republic of Albania and the Soviet Union in the early 1960s. The greater distance between Albania and the Soviet Union also had important consequences for the quality of the education of architects in the country. The first Albanian university (the University of Tirana) was founded in 1957, which meant that some students who had just finished their studies in other Eastern European countries immediately became lecturers on their return to Albania. I think the resulting gaps in theoretical background are also one of the main reasons for the lack of serious literature on the achievements of socialist architecture in Albania.

Jonas: What role did architects play in the political system of the Socialist Republic?

Dritan: Being an architect in the Socialist Republic was not a privilege, as you were very limited in your work. Architects had little importance for the political elite. In 1957 for instance, there was a meeting of artistic practitioners, writers, painters etc., which was organised by the LAWA, the League of Albanian Writers and Artists, an organisation which also incorporated architects. But at this meeting there was no architect present and when the former Minister of Interior Affairs brought up the absence of architects, the answer of dictator Enver Hoxha was: "[...] they have not made enough of an impression on our national architecture, so we do not need them to be here." Also, for an architect, there was always a risk of a sudden end of his or her career through the authorities if what they said was not in accordance with party doctrine. You could easily be downgraded and banned to the periphery. I also consider the presence of Italy in the first half of the 20th century in Albania an important influence in terms of modernisation of the country. The Italians brought modern technology and urban planning with them.

Jonas: What were the party's guidelines in terms of housing?

Dritan: The party's attitude in the construction sector for the whole socialist period can be described by the slogan "faster, cheaper, better". "Faster" expresses the idea that Albania's slower development in comparison with the rest of Europe represented a desire to catch up with building developments quickly. Building "cheaper" was the only way forward for a country with an underdeveloped economy, like Albania. Foreign aid—first from the Soviet Union, later from China—was a constraint to economic growth, thus a later strategy of self-reliance had fatal consequences for Albania's economy. And thirdly "better" indicates an aspiration to construct beautiful buildings.

There is an obvious inner contradiction between constructing fast and cheap buildings on one hand, and better buildings on the other hand. And, as I said before, one must consider the position that architects held during the years of the socialist regime in order to understand the actual architectural possibilities. The party's standpoint was often ambivalent in these regards and sometimes a clear point of view simply did not exist.

However, there is an article in the party's monthly magazine *Rruga e Partise* (Party's Path) from 1974, in which the author Shinasi Dragoti—the then Minister of Construction—describes the party's guidelines in terms of aesthetics in architecture. The article is entitled "Issues of aesthetics in architecture" and explains that socialist architecture must be characterised by simplicity, and modern architecture should be the basis and an example for anything that follows. The principles of ideal composition are to be found in simple forms, line harmony and clear structure. He also points out that a national design is considered fundamental for the principle of a new architecture. Architects, instead of borrowing form, elements and details from the past, should study the country's tradition in order to attain a better understanding of historic residential areas, detect these components of urban transformation and influences and give an appropriate response to these demands.

Jonas: Are there aspects of the socialist architecture where you see a link to the informal building in Tirana after the end of the Socialist Republic?

Dritan: Although the socialist era as a concluded political chapter has ended, it is important to take a closer look at this era in order to reach a deeper understanding of the present city of Tirana. I also think that in order to understand both socialist and current building practices, we need to extend our view to a sociological, cultural, and psychological perspective. In that sense I see the informal building in the 1990s as a consequence of total state control over building practice during socialism. The possibility to extend an apartment when there is a need for it was a freedom that never existed in the socialist state. However, from an architectural point of view, the modern town of Tirana —seen as a morphological unit—is full of voids. While the historic town achieved its density over centuries, in the Socialist Republic the density of Tirana was controlled by the state. So in a way it is these gaps—resulting from socialist building and policy—that made the rapid increase of density since the 1990s possible. During the socialist era, commercial activities were limited and social life was controlled, whereas today you see a vibrant city full of commercial activity. From this point of view I see more parallels between today's Tirana and the Ottoman town, whose origin is the bazaar.

Jonas: So the socialist structure of the city with its voids was a reason for the rapid transformation of the city?

Dritan: Yes. But I also think, that Albania has a somewhat problematic relation with time. As already mentioned, during the 20th century Albania's main goal was to achieve the same pace of modernisation as the rest of Europe. But one should bear in mind that Albania went straight from a feudalist society to a socialist model. And today a certain haste to keep up with other European countries is noticeable —however, being in a hurry often leads to mistakes. I am sure that there is a lot to learn from the past, from achievements as well as from failures. It is a recurrent phenomenon, especially in transitory periods, that a strict dividing line is drawn under the preceding era: whilst Modernism used an aggressive language to establish a clear distinction from Neo-Classicism, the same happens today with the socialist past. It is therefore necessary to study past experiences and to look beyond ideologies of the moment in order to enable a dialogue between different periods. I see this as a great contribution scholars can give to society.

Marrëdhënie: Negotiate is to have a Relationship

Jonas von Lenthe in conversation with Simon Battisti on the implications of culture on the built environment. The interview took place at the Palace of Culture of Tirana in March 2015.

Jonas: How long have you been in Tirana and what was your motive for coming here?

Simon: I came to Tirana for the first time in February 2014. Six months earlier I had become interested in a master plan by Grimshaw Architects that proposed to extend the main boulevard of the city toward Paskuqan, an informal neighbourhood north of the city, which is now part of the Tirana Municipality (the country's municipal borders were redrawn in 2015). I thought the project stirred up a lot of interesting questions about the city. Tirana was established as a "formal" city in the 1920s through the gesture of building a boulevard. And Grimshaw's idea to extend it re-opens a very long history of these types of proposals. Over the past century there have been something like seventy official master plans commissioned for Tirana, most of which focus on the boulevard. It remains an overpowering element in the city.

Historically, Tirana is an obsessively planned and replanned city, despite the general agreement that it is a "chaotic city". This situation fascinated me. My thesis project at Harvard was a proposal intervening at the scale of big buildings instead of that of a master plan. Specifically, long, low buildings. This typology has interesting precedence here, and I was very interested in addressing Tirana's love affair with linearity in a way that avoided demolition as a kind of requisite, parallel act to construction. As soon as I finished grad school, I came back to Tirana on a grant to continue research on the city. Today I am working and living here as an independent architect, still fascinated by the city every day.

Jonas: My first impression of Tirana was, as you said, that it is a very chaotic city. However, the more time I spend here, the closer I get to discovering a deeper order. What is your perception of how Tirana is structured?

Simon: At first sight Tirana is quite chaotic and difficult to understand. But when you take a closer look, you basically find four typologies of residential buildings. There is the original vernacular house, there are the Italian-era villas from the 1930s that dot the city, there are the socialist housing blocks, which have a number of interesting construction typologies, but with pretty regular siting strategies throughout the city, and with a kind of singular presence wherever you find them, and then there are the apartment buildings that were built after 1991. They tend to be point-loaded towers between six and twelve floors tall. Each of these types is of course a kind of demonstration of the ways of living and predominant social modes at the time when they were built. When one explores the city on foot, this fairly even distribution of the different typologies is obvious.

Jonas: Your research is about informal construction methods. What are you focusing on at the moment?

Simon: I am really interested in construction finance in Tirana, especially the role of banks, or the lack of banks, in the development process—even of big buildings twenty floors tall. When I came to Tirana to do research for my thesis, the people I was meeting kept using this term "swap", which means that a developer wants to build a large building and does not have the cash to pay for it. And in the 1990s in Albania there was no credit available from banks for construction. What emerged was a practice of informal lending, where apartments in these buildings were used as currency to pay for raw materials and services like labor and even the design. So construction could take place without cash because the suppliers of bricks, concrete, etc., would receive payment in the form of an apartment. This could get complex, of course, especially when developers needed imported goods like windows. In that case it could involve a number of other trades with third or fourth parties because at some point cash was required.

Jonas: What are the origins of this financing method?

Simon: After the fall of socialism, all of a sudden anybody with a truck could become rich. You could drive to Italy and buy used TVs or washing machines and instantly sell them in Albania; there was an insatiable demand for goods from "outside". Huge money was made from importing goods. Some of the richest people in Albania today started by importing appliances one truck at a time. It was a free-for-all because it was a cash system. With regard to buildings, you could either keep your cash under your mattress with the risk that at any moment it could become worthless, or convert it into something more stable, like a building. Remittances played a huge role in this too, as individuals working abroad could invest money in their home country to support their families. A building was the most secure place to put money. I have a friend here whose father was an architect, and for years he was paid in apartments. By the early 2000s the family had accumulated something like twenty apartments. And it was payment for all kinds of services. But by the 2000s, the "swap" boom had died down somewhat. The first lending to individuals started around 2002. And this obviously changed a lot for both homebuyers and developers.

Jonas: Is this financing system the cause of Tirana's density?

Simon: I think it is a big part of the story, yes. Buildings became such important currency because they were not just a place to save your money but a place to make even more money. This means much of Tirana was not built to satisfy a need for housing per se, but as an investment by individuals to retain his or her own wealth. Much of the city is quite densely built, but occupation can be very low. There are no exact numbers on this, but many buildings and apartments in the city are unoccupied and empty.

Jonas: Is "swap" still part of the development process when a building is built in Tirana today?

Simon: No, "swap" does not happen in Tirana anymore because land ownership has become regulated.

Jonas: How about the property ownership in socialist housing blocks? Do inhabitants normally own their apartment?

Simon: Yes, everything is privatised today. There is a small number of subsidised apartments in Tirana, something like 500 total, although this is something the city is interested in expanding.

Jonas: I have the impression that the transition between two political and cultural systems produced its own logic. It seems that people immediately adopted capitalist mechanisms, but their own informal interpretation of it.

Simon: Yes, it is very interesting how capitalism is received in Albania, how the transition is happening. As you said, it can often appear that, on the one hand, there is an immediate embracing of capitalism. On the other hand, I am really interested in how there might be another kind of narrative—which is that there is a cultural history that rejects some important aspects of capitalism.

One of these rejections, or incongruities, between everyday capitalism and Albanian culture is the nuanced forms of negotiation that occur between individuals. Face-to-face interaction is deeply important in this context. There is an Albanian word, "marrëdhënië", which means negotiation. It is a composite of "to take" (marr) and "to give" (dhënie). Albanians will joke that the "take" comes before the "give" here. But "marrëdhënie" is also the word for relationship. You use it when speaking about your lover, friend or your brother or sister. So to have a relationship is to negotiate, and to negotiate is to have a relationship. In this context then, one can see how something like "swap" is quite an obvious solution, in that it fulfills a certain desire for give and take. People are very willing to enter into agreements with one another without the involvement of banks or lawyers. There is an incredibly strong trust put in one's word; it means everything. For me, it was a fascinating idea that there is something so tangible on a cultural level that has implications on the very physical reality of the built environment.

Even after credit became available here, there were and continue to be deep suspicions about institutions like banks. The collapse of the economy in 1997 contributed a lot to this. So when in the culture there is a pretty deep understanding that the basis of a deal is “marrëdhënie” and that constitutes its legitimacy and so on, there is a kind of automatic suspicion and resistance to dealing with a bank.

Jonas: So if banks are not welcome in the development process, what about architects? Do they play a role?

Simon: Architects are crucial here! They may not be very well treated by their clients, and their work is not considered to have much real influence in the conversation about public space, but they have played a huge role in Tirana inasmuch as they have been used to channel the visual fashions of the “West”—they have done the technical work of transforming the limited local materials into an international visual language. In a way, it is a project of translation. Today, tools like Pinterest have become standard for designers, and there are many interiors in Tirana that seamlessly reproduce the international flavor of lifestyle design that is so rich on Pinterest. For instance, in the early 2000s the “piano bar” was a very popular kind of business here, although this is now completely out of fashion. But it would have been the architect’s responsibility to create a convincing environment like that. This year has been the year of the “jazz café”. I could probably name eight cafés that have opened or rebranded themselves in this mold since September and architects or designers would have been involved in these, too.

Jonas: Is the aim of your research to learn from informality and maybe incorporate parts of it into your own practice as an architect?

Simon: Much of what I have spoken about are practices and habits that are deeply embedded in Albanian culture and I am not interested in adapting them into my own practice per se. Yet I am interested in how culture and the built environment reflect one another. There is much truth in the cliché that cities are expressions of human achievement or desire. The built environment is an expression of culture and this idea feels quite accessible in Tirana, as it is so visible.

Jonas: Are there examples of public spaces that were designed informally by a group of inhabitants together?

Simon: One of my favorite public spaces in Tirana is an informal one! If you look at a map of Tirana, there is a large open space north of the boulevard, where the train tracks curve south into Tirana and terminate at what used to be the central train station. This open space was farmland during socialism. When Tirana rapidly expanded with informal houses on the periphery, somehow this one enormous space was never filled. Almost the entirety of the fields surrounding Tirana are packed and yet this strip remains. It is very curious. And it has this effortlessly diverse mixture of uses that is quite beautiful. It is a pedestrian highway connecting Paskuqan, the neighbour-hood we spoke about at the beginning of our conversation, to Tirana. There is a constant stream of people walking there until pretty late at night. Then there are grazing cows, there are second hand clothes stalls perched on these little mounds of grass along the path, and there are kids playing soccer all over the place across the flat open spaces. The terrain is kind of wavy, there are these long mounds, but everything is covered in a soft grass, and the kids run up and over them even with the soccer ball. And then finally there are the enormous electrical high-voltage lines that were added recently because it was the only open space left in the city. On a sunny day it is truly an amazing space. It is one of the many places in Albania where you can squint and almost see something utopian, and yet there is some-thing just as easily apocalyptic about it. Maybe that is true about Tirana itself.

Interview Partners

Simon Battisti,
born 1983 in the USA, is an architect and educator based in Tirana, Albania. He was curator of the Albanian Pavilion at the 2016 Venice Biennale of Architecture. From 2014 to 2015 he was a Fulbright Fellow in Albania, and a visiting lecturer at Epoka University's Department of Architecture. He holds a Master's degree in Architecture from Harvard University Graduate School of Design, where he co-founded the student journal *Very Vary Veri.* He writes regularly about architecture and urbanism, and is the editor of *Flexible Leviathan: Reconsidering Scale and Fixity in Iztapalapa, Mexico City* (Harvard GSD, 2016). He has worked in design offices in Los Angeles, Mumbai, and New York City.

Ledian Bregasi,
born 1984 in Albania, is an architect based in Tirana and Rome. He has published several articles about informal architecture, such as "An Architecture without Architects" (In: *Theory for the Sake of the Theory: ARCHTHEO'11 Conference Proceedings,* 2011) and "Self regulation as a Tool for the Management of the Complexity in Architecture" (In: *Civilisation at the Crossroads, Response and Responsibility of the Systems Sciences, Book of Abstracts of the European Meetings on Cybernetics and Systems Research,* 2014). He holds a PhD from the Sapienza University of Rome. The title of his PhD thesis is *Emergent properties as an instrument for management of complexity in architecture.*

Dritan Mico,
born 1975 in Albania, is an architect based in Rome. He has worked in different architectural offices in Italy and Greece and has published several articles about Albanian socialist architecture, such as "When Words Fall on Deaf Ears–An Outline of Albania's Socialist Architecture" (In: *sITA Volume 1,* 2013). He holds a PhD from the Sapienza University of Rome. The title of his PhD thesis is *Gaps to be filled. How socialist modernity has shaped Albanian society and architecture within an endless transition.*

The pictures on p. 23, p. 29, p. 32, p. 41 p. 47, p. 48, p. 55 were part of the “Arkivi Qendror Teknik i Nderimit” (AQTN; Central Technical Archive of Construction). They show housing blocks in Tirana right after their construction was finished. The pictures were taken between 1958 and 1970.

The pictures on p. 71, p. 74, p. 81, p. 82, p. 89 were taken by inhabitants of their houses in order to send them to the “Agjencia e legalizimit urbanizimit dhe integrimit te zonave ndertimeve informale” (ALUIZNI; the public Albanian agency that is in charge of the legalisation of informal buildings and areas), as part of the application for the legalisation of their home.

All other pictures shown in this book were taken by Jonas von Lenthe in March 2015 in and around Tirana, Albania.

Responding to Particular Needs at a Precise Moment

The author would like to thank for their support:
Joni Baboci, Simon Battisti, Bless, Ledian Bregasi, Felix Buchholz, Verena Buttmann, Bettina D'Cruz, Lisiena Dimo, Besmira Dyca, Andreas Hemming, Johannes Hucht, Jason King, David Laflamme, Olesja Lami, Armin Linke, Dritan Mico, Andreas Müller, Carlo Siegfried, Elisabetta Terragni, Tirana Ekspres, Jan Wenzel, Jonas Zilius, Deutsch-Albanische Freundschaftsgesellschaft

The choice of only male interview partners is unintentional and results from an undirected information search. Although not discussed in this book, it is important to discuss whether this dominance reflects the gender ratio and hierarchy within the field of architecture.

Photography: Jonas von Lenthe
Interviews: Jonas von Lenthe with Simon Battisti, Ledian Bregasi and Dritan Mico
Concept: Jonas von Lenthe
Design: Johannes Hucht
Proofreading: Bettina D'Cruz, Jason King
Lithography: Christian Ertel
Printing: Pöge Druck, Leipzig

Paper: Bavaria Bulk 90g/qm, Euroboard Spezial Gt 300g/qm

Published by:
Spector Books,
Harkortstraße 10, 04107 Leipzig

Distribution:
Germany, Austria: GVA, Gemeinsame Verlagsauslieferung Göttingen GmbH & Co. KG, www.gva-verlage.de
Switzerland: AVA Verlagsauslieferung AG, www.ava.ch
France, Belgium: Interart Paris, www.interart.fr
UK: Central Books Ltd, www.centralbooks.com
South Korea: The Book Society, www.thebooksociety.org
Australia, New Zealand: Perimeter Distribution, www.perimeterdistribution.com

Kindly supported by Freundeskreis der HFBK Hamburg e.V.

First Edition: 2018
ISBN 978-3-95905-208-5